Presented to

Christy

From

Roberta

On the Occasion of

Happy Birthday!

Date

May 25, 2006

DAILY WISDOM

for

MOTHERS

Encouragement for Every Day

MICHELLE MEDLOCK ADAMS

BARBOUR

Cover image © Getty Images

Design: UDG | DesignWorks, Sisters, Oregon

Published by Barbour Publishing, Inc., P.O. Box 719, Uhrichsville, Ohio 44683
www.barbourbooks.com

*Our mission is to publish and distribute inspirational products offering exceptional value and
biblical encouragement to the masses.*

Member of the
Evangelical Christian
Publishers Association

Printed in China.
5 4 3 2 1

For my mother, MARION, who is full of wisdom.

Thanks for always believing in me.

And for my mother-in-law, MARTHA.

Thanks for raising such a wonderful son.

I love you both!

Michelle (a.k.a. Missy)

INTRODUCTION

Let's face it. Life is busy—especially for moms. As a mother of two young girls, I find it challenging some days just to make time for a shower, let alone time to spend with God. I'm sure you face the same thing—you desire a deeper relationship with the Lord, but you don't have hours to spend in His Word every day.

That's why this book is perfect for moms like us. I wrote it with you in mind. Within these pages you'll find a quick, easy-to-read devotional. A Scripture and a short prayer complete each reading. We'll tackle different aspects of being a mom and hopefully become stronger and wiser in every area of our lives!

I hope that you'll look forward to your devotional time each day. Grab a Diet Coke or a cup of java and spend some time with God today. Maybe you can squeeze it in while the kiddos are napping. Or maybe your best time with God is right after you put the children to bed at night. It doesn't really matter—whenever you sit down with this book, it'll be the right time. I pray that God will open your eyes and your heart as we take this journey together.

MICHELLE MEDLOCK ADAMS

REST FOR MOMS

"Come to me,
all you who are weary and burdened,
and I will give you rest."

MATTHEW 11:28

Ahhh. . .rest. Who wouldn't love a day of rest? But let's face it. Mothers don't really get a day of rest. If we rested, who would fix breakfast? Who would get the children ready for church? Who would do the laundry so your son can wear his lucky socks for the big game on Monday?

No, there's not a lot of rest in a mother's schedule. But, that's not really the kind of rest this verse is talking about. The rest mentioned in this verse is the kind of rest that only Jesus can provide. Resting in Jesus means feeling secure in Him and allowing His peace to fill your soul. That kind of rest is available to all—even mothers.

So, in the midst of the hustle and bustle of your life (even if you're elbow deep in dishwater), you can rest in Him. Start by meditating on the Lord's promises and His everlasting love for you. Make a mental list of the things in your life that you are thankful for, and praise God for each one. Allow His love to overwhelm you. . .and rest.

MOM TO MASTER

Lord, help me to rest in You—even when I'm overwhelmed with the "to-dos" of each day. I want more of You in my life. I love You. Amen.

CASTING YOUR CARES

Cast all your anxiety on him
because he cares for you.
1 PETER 5:7

Ever have one of those days? The alarm clock didn't go off. The kids were late for school. The dog threw up on the carpet. You spilled coffee down the front of your new white blouse. Ahhh! It's one of those "Calgon, take me away!" days, right?

But it doesn't have to be. No matter how many challenges you face today, you can smile in the face of aggravation. How? By casting your cares upon the Lord. That's what the Lord tells us to do in His Word, yet many of us feel compelled to take all of the cares upon ourselves. After all, we're mothers. We're fixers. We're the doers of

the bunch. We wear five or six fedoras at a time—
we can handle anything that comes our way, right?

Wrong! But God can. When the day starts to
go south, cast your cares on Him. He wants you
to! As mothers, we can handle a lot, but it's true
what they say—Father really does know best. So,
give it to God. C'mon, you know you want to. . . .

MOM TO MASTER
*Lord, help me to turn to You when my troubles seem
too big to face alone, and even when they don't.
Help me to trust You with all of my cares. I love You,
Lord. Amen.*

GOD HAS A PLAN

"For I know the plans I have for you,"
declares the LORD, *"plans to prosper you and not to harm*
you, plans to give you hope and a future."
JEREMIAH 29:11

Do you ever feel like you're not doing enough for your children? Sure, you enrolled them in ballet, karate, and gymnastics, but you forgot to sign them up for soccer— and now it's too late! The recording in your head begins playing, "You're a bad mother."

I hear that same recording. Sometimes it plays nonstop.

I worry that I'm not providing my children with the opportunities that will bring success. What if they don't make the middle school soccer team because I didn't sign them up for summer soccer camp? What if they miss out on those academic scholarships because I didn't spend enough time reading with them when they were little?

What if? What if? What if?

You know, God doesn't want us dwelling in the land of "What If." He wants us to trust Him with our children. He wants us to quit "what if-ing!" God has a plan for their lives—better than you could ever imagine. So, relax. You're not a bad mother because you missed soccer camp sign-ups. If you've given your children to God, you've given them the best chance to succeed that you could ever give them!

MOM TO MASTER

Lord, I give my children to You. Thank You, God, for Your plans. Amen.

Miss America Moms

I'm sure you know her. She's the mom who has a flat belly, long legs, and perfect hair. Admit it, you occasionally wish she'd fall into a cotton candy

machine and gain thirty pounds. Her very presence makes you feel less than attractive, doesn't it?

Guess how I know these things? Because I know a Miss America mom, too, and I feel like one of Cinderella's ugly stepsisters whenever she's around.

Comparing yourself with others is never a good thing, and it's not a God thing, either. God isn't concerned with whether or not your belly is as trim as it was before childbirth. His Word says that He looks on the heart, not on your outward appearance. He's more concerned with the condition of your heart, not the cellulite on your legs. Of course, that doesn't mean we shouldn't strive to be the best we can be—both inside and out—but it certainly relieves some of that pressure to be perfect.

Give your jealousies and feelings of inadequacy to God and find your identity in Him. He loves you just the way you are—even if you're not Miss America.

MOM TO MASTER
Father, help me not to compare myself with others. Help me to see myself through Your eyes. Amen.

Stop, Pause, and Praise

You shall rejoice in all the good things
the LORD your God has given
to you and your household.

DEUTERONOMY 26:11

"Rejoice in the Lord always. Again I will say,
rejoice!" (Philippians 4:4 NKJV). That's what
the Word says, but that's not always the easiest
task. . .am I right? What about when your child's
teacher says something ugly about Junior during
your parent/teacher conference? Or, how about
when another driver pulls right in front of you
and steals your parking spot at the grocery store?
Or when your toddler knocks over your red
fingernail polish, spilling it all over your bathroom
rug? Not wanting to rejoice too much at that
point, are you?

Daily aggravations will be a part of life until
we get to heaven. That's a fact. So, we just have to
learn how to deal with those aggravations.

Here's the plan: Today if something goes wrong—stop, pause, and praise. I don't mean you have to praise God for the aggravation. That would be kind of silly. I'm saying just praise God *in spite of* the aggravation. Before long, the "stop, pause, and praise" practice will become a habit. And that's the kind of habit worth forming! So go on, start rejoicing!

MOM TO MASTER

Father, I repent for the times when I am less than thankful. I rejoice in You today. Amen.

Go to God

"Martha, Martha," the Lord answered,
"you are worried and upset about many things,
but only one thing is needed. Mary has chosen what
is better, and it will not be taken away from her."

LUKE 10:41–42

Do you remember when you were pregnant?
In the midst of weird food cravings, swollen
ankles, and raging hormones, you spent time
dreaming of your baby. You wondered things like:
"What will he or she look like?" "What will be his
or her first words?" "Will he or she be healthy?"
and "How will I ever care for a tiny little baby?"

I think every mother worries. It seems like
the natural thing to do. Most first-time moms
worry that they won't be equipped with the
appropriate parenting skills needed to be a good
mom. Then the baby comes—and with it, a
whole new set of worries. As the child grows,
the worries grow, too. Sometimes the worries
can become almost suffocating.

When I feel overwhelmed with the worries that accompany motherhood, I realize I've forgotten to figure God into the equation. With God, all things are possible—even raising good kids in a mixed-up world. God doesn't expect mothers to have all the answers, but He does expect us to go to Him for those answers. So, if worries are consuming your thoughts—go to God. He not only has the answers, He is the answer!

MOM TO MASTER

God, I trust You with my children, and I give You my worries. Amen.

A LIFELONG FRIEND

Dear children,
do not let anyone lead you astray.

1 JOHN 3:7

D
o you ever worry about the friends that your children are making? I do. I often wonder, *Will they be good influences on my children? Will they hurt my children? Do they know Jesus as their Lord and Savior? Will they be lifelong, trustworthy friends?*

While I don't know the answers to all of these questions, I do know one thing—Jesus will be their lifelong friend. They will always be able to count on Him. He will come through for them time and time again. He will stand by them no matter what. How do I know these things? Because He's been there for me when nobody else was.

I discovered early in life that friends sometimes let you down—even your best friends—because they're human. If you put your hope in friends, disappointment and hurt are inevitable. But God is a sure thing.

I realize that I can't pick my children's friends, and I know that I can't protect them from the hurt that comes from broken friendships and disloyalty. But there are two things I can do—I can teach them about Jesus, and I can pray that the Lord sends them godly friends. You can do the same for your kids. You can start today.

Mom to Master

Lord, please send my children good friends. I'm thankful that You're their best friend and mine. Amen.

HAND IT OVER

"Therefore I tell you,
do not worry about your life."
MATTHEW 6:25

It amazes me sometimes just how much I worry.
The Bible clearly says to cast all of your cares
on Him, yet I choose to keep those cares to
myself. By nature, I'm a fixer; I'm a doer. And
sometimes that works against me. While my self-
sufficient nature enables me to get a lot
accomplished, it also causes me to worry over
things that I should hand over to God.

Are you a worrier, too? To some extent,
I think all moms are worriers. Worrying just
seems to be part of our job description, right
underneath the "take care of your children until
you die" part. While worrying may come naturally
to you, it's not God's will for your life. He wants
you to live in perfect peace, and worrying is a
peace destroyer. It's the opposite of peace. So, why
not give your worries to God today?

It won't be easy at first, but you can do it.
Here's the plan: The very minute that your

thoughts turn into worries, say aloud, "I cast (fill in the blank) on God right now." Pretty soon, casting your cares will become a habit and worrying will be a thing of the past.

MOM TO MASTER

Father, transform my thinking. Help me to quit worrying and simply trust You with every part of my life. Amen.

CELEBRATE YOUR CHILDREN

*"My grace is sufficient for you,
for my power is made perfect in weakness."*

2 CORINTHIANS 12:9

It's the mother's curse. I'm sure your mom has used it on you before: "I hope you have a child just like you when you grow up!" And, chances are—you did! In my case, I had two. You know what's interesting about raising children that are exactly like you? You tend to see all of your faults in them. It's as if there is a gigantic magnifying glass, constantly revealing their weaknesses, which happen to be the same weaknesses that you struggle with on a daily basis.

This, of course, is the breeding ground for fighting, resentment, and hurt. So, as mothers, we have to break that "mother's curse" and celebrate our children. We need to smash that magnifying glass that focuses in on their flaws and love our kids—weaknesses and all. Ask the Lord

to help you see your children as God sees them.
And, ask Him to help you see yourself through
His eyes, too.

In other words, give your kids and yourself a
break. Don't expect them to be perfect, and don't
expect perfection from yourself, either. God loves
you and your kids—flaws and all. Remember,
His power is made perfect through our weakness.

Mom to Master

*Lord, help me to nurture my children's strengths and
pray over their weaknesses. I give them to You. Amen.*

LOVE IS THE ANSWER

God is love.
Whoever lives in love lives in God,
and God in him. In this way,
love is made complete among us.

1 JOHN 4:16–17

Remember that popular '70s song "Love Will Keep Us Together"? I was in grade school when it hit the radio airwaves, and I can remember singing it at recess with my gal pals. We knew every word by heart. Well, there's a lot of truth in that title, especially where our families are concerned.

Life gets complicated, and families fall apart. It happens. It even happens to Christian families. It may have happened in your own family. But I'm here to tell you that love is the answer. When nothing else will, love will keep your family together. No, I'm not talking about that fair-weather kind of love. I'm talking about the God kind of love—an everlasting, unconditional love from heaven.

So, even if your teenager has left home or turned his back on God, love will draw him back.

Not the sermons you've preached nor the rules you've enforced—only love will turn your situation around. Let God's love live big in you. Let God's love be the superglue in your family, binding you with one another for a lifetime. Live the love and reap the results.

MOM TO MASTER
Father, I ask that Your love flow through me to my children. Amen.

An Everlasting Love

I trust in God's unfailing love for ever and ever.

PSALM 52:8

We use the word *love* an awful lot. "I *love* your new purse," or "I *love* that dress on you," or "I *love* Hershey kisses." I bet if you kept track, you'd find yourself using the word *love* more than a dozen times each day. Because we use it so much, love has lost some of its punch, some of its luster, some of its meaning.

But real love—the God kind of love—is so much more than the "love" that has become so clichéd in our culture. The God kind of love is an everlasting love. His love stretches as far as the east is from the west. His love is deeper than the deepest ocean. His love is higher than the highest mountain. His love covers a multitude of sins. His love is unconditional. His love is truly awesome!

Now, that's the kind of love I want to walk in. How about you? I want to receive the Father's love, and I want to extend His love to others—especially to my children. As moms, we should have the aroma of love. So, if your love aroma is a little funky (like that green cheese in the back of the fridge), ask God to refresh your love today!

Mom to Master

Lord, I pray that Your love—the real thing—shines in me and through me. Amen.

WALKING IN LOVE

I trust in God's unfailing love
for ever and ever.

PSALM 52:8

Sometimes it's harder to walk in love than others. Can I get an "Amen!" on that? There are days when my love walk has quite a limp. On those days, I often wonder how God can still love me. Ever wondered that yourself? I'll think back over something I've said or done that was less than lovely, and my insides cringe.

This is especially true when it comes to my children. Of all the people in my life, I want to make sure I show my kids that unconditional, always-there-for-you kind of love. So, when I fail to accomplish that goal, my heart hurts. But it's in those times that I sense the Father's presence in a big way. I can literally feel His love wrapping around me like a cozy sweater.

No matter how many times I fail, God still loves me. And, on those days when I know I'm definitely not in the running for "Mother of the Year," that's good to know. God loves us even more than we love our children. In fact, the Word says that we're the apple of His eye. I like that. So, the next time your love walk becomes more of a crawl, remember—God adores you.

Mom to Master

Heavenly Father, thank You for loving me even when I am less than loving. Amen.

GROWING IN LOVE

[Love] is not self-seeking.
1 CORINTHIANS 13:5

Love means putting others' needs and desires before your own. Of course, as moms, we are well aware of that fact. When my girls were toddlers, they had many needs and desires. In fact, it seemed that one of them needed something from me all the time. If I had taken a shower by 3 p.m., I was doing well.

Especially when our children are little, we get to learn firsthand that aspect of love. And some days it's not easy. There were times when I prayed, "Please, God, just let them nap at the same time today so I can take a long, hot bath." (Hey, I would've paid a thousand dollars for a bubble bath back then!) Those were precious times, but boy, they were busy times, too!

Maybe you're living those busy days right now. Maybe you're reading this and thinking, "Precious days? I want to escape!" Well, don't despair. God cares about your crazy, busy days. He knows that this "mom gig" isn't an easy job. He wants to give you rest and peace, and He is well pleased with your well doing. So, the next time you hear "Mommy!" and you want to run the other direction—take heart! You are growing in love.

MOM TO MASTER
Lord, help me to appreciate even the busiest of days, and help me to show Your love today. Amen.

A DAILY LOVE LETTER

"For I, the LORD your God,
am a jealous God."

EXODUS 20:5

Remember your first love? I married my high school sweetheart. I remember the first time we held hands. I remember the first time we kissed. I remember the exact outfit I was wearing when he first said he loved me. I remember it all! Even after twelve years of marriage, I still smile and get all sappy when I hear "our song" on the radio.

God wants us to love Him even more than we love our spouse and children. He tells us that He is a jealous God. He wants us to remember those special times with Him—the moment you gave your heart to Him, the miracles He has performed in your life, the times He came through when no one else could. . . . He wants us to sing praise songs to Him as a love offering. He says if we won't praise

Him, the rocks will cry out. I don't want any rock doing my praising for me. How about you?

Start today and keep an "I Remember" journal. Record what God does for you each day—even the smallest things. It'll be sort of a daily "love letter" to the Father. If you've grown cold to God, you're sure to fall in love with Him again.

MOM TO MASTER

Lord, help me to keep You as my first love. Amen.

TIME, NOT MONEY

Jesus said, "Let the little children come to me,
and do not hinder them."

MATTHEW 19:14

I once read an article that said children spell love
T-I-M-E. As I pondered that statement, I had to
agree. Sometimes, as parents, we think that our
kids spell love M-O-N-E-Y because our society
has become so materialistic, but in reality, kids
just want to be with us. Abby and Ally would
rather spend an afternoon watching old Doris Day
movies on my big bed than practically anything I
could give them. They actually enjoy being with
me, and that's something I am so thankful for.
I realize that as they get older, that may not always
be true, so I want to take advantage of each and
every opportunity to snuggle together, eat buttery
popcorn, and watch Doris Day work her onscreen
magic with Rock Hudson.

Find some activities that you and your
children enjoy doing together like going hiking,
going fishing, doing crafts, reading stories, baking
cookies, playing board games. . . Just find some

common ground and make time for your children. Even if you have to "pencil in" a day of baking cookies with kids in your daily planner—do it! Don't just say you love your children—show them! Spend some time together.

Mom to Master

Father, I want to thank You for every moment I get to spend with my children. Help me to treasure this time. Amen.

OPEN YOUR EARS

Let the wise listen
and add to their learning.

PROVERBS 1:5

L istening. It's almost a lost art form in today's
world. Yet, according to the International
Listening Association, "Being listened to spells the
difference between feeling accepted and feeling
isolated." Wow, that's pretty strong, isn't it?

In professional circles, I am a good listener.
I understand the importance of listening to my
colleagues; yet I sometimes fail to listen to my
children. I find myself interrupting them, trying to
get them to "get to the end of the story" while I am
still young. But that's not what I should be doing as
a caring, accepting mom. The Lord convicted me
about this very thing not long ago, and I've been
working on my listening skills ever since.

Are you a good listener? Do you really give your kids your full attention when they are talking to you? Do you nod your head and smile, letting them know that you're truly into what they are saying? If not, you may need to ask God to help you improve your listening skills, too. If we fail to listen to them now, we'll be sorry later when they no longer choose to tell us things. So, go ahead. Open up your ears and your heart and listen to your children!

Mom to Master

Lord, please help me to listen to my children the same way that You listen to me. Amen.

SOAKING IN THE PEACE

Oh, how I love your law!
I meditate on it all day long.

PSALM 119:97

Don't you just love to soak in a big bathtub
full of bubbles? The beautiful bubbles tickle
your toes, and the fresh, flowery fragrance fills the
room. It's one of my most favorite things to do.
If I could, I would soak in the tub so long that my
entire body would become "pruney." There's just
nothing like a bubble bath—it's pure heaven!
It's time well spent, as far as I'm concerned.
Soaking in bubbles totally de-stresses me and
brings a quiet rest to my soul. And what mom
doesn't need more of that in her life?

Do you know what else brings peace and rest?
Soaking in God's Word. When you spend time in
the Word of God, it transforms you from the
inside out. It replaces stress with peace; sickness
with healing; anger with compassion; hate with

love; worry with faith; and weariness with energy. Soaking in God's Word every day will keep you balanced and ready to tackle whatever comes your way. It's time well spent. You'll become a better person—a better wife and a better mom. And you won't even get "pruney" in the process.

Mom to Master

Lord, thank You for Your Word. Help me to soak it in more and more each day. Amen.

MAKING MEMORIES

"By this all men will know that you are my disciples,
if you love one another."

JOHN 13:35

When was the last time you slowed down
long enough to make mud pies with your
kids? When was the last time you read funny
poetry by a candlelight pizza dinner? If it's been
awhile, then plan a special day to do nothing but

fun stuff with your children. Of course, this works much better if your kids are willing to spend an entire day with you. Once they reach puberty, Mom is sort of on the "nerd list." But if you still have little ones or tweens running around, why not host an all-out fun-filled day?

Begin with pizza for breakfast. Watch funny family films in your jammies until noon. Then, if the weather is nice, take a bike ride together or go on a scavenger hunt in a nearby park. Play board games until nightfall. Finish the day with devotions and prayer time. Just bask in each other's presence, soaking it all in.

At the end of the day, you will have made some magnificent memories. When your kids are old, they'll look back on that day and smile. They may not remember exactly what you did, but they'll remember the love.

MOM TO MASTER
Lord, help me to spend more quality time with my family. Amen.

NEGATIVE NELLIE

Jesus said,
"Let the little children come to me,
and do not hinder them."

MATTHEW 19:14

N o."
That was always the answer I received from one of my former bosses. No matter what idea I'd offer—even if it had been the best suggestion in the world—his answer was always "No." I nicknamed him "Negative Ned." Though I tried to joke about it, his negativity almost crippled me on the inside.

After being shot down so many times, I quit offering suggestions. I quit sharing my thoughts. I went into my "survival mode" with all of my defenses up. God eventually freed me from that supervisor, but I learned a lot during those months of drifting in the Sea of Negativism. Those lessons have stayed with me, and I often think of Old Ned when I'm parenting.

As moms, it seems our duty to say no. And sometimes no is the correct response. But don't be so quick to always say no, or your children will quit asking you stuff. They'll go into their survival mode and put up their defenses— just like I did with my boss. As moms, we should take time to really listen to our kids' requests before saying no. If we don't, we just might become "Negative Nellie."

MOM TO MASTER
Lord, help me to be open-minded and approachable— especially with my children. Amen.

KIDS AS TEACHERS

*Don't let anyone look down on you
because you are young.*

1 TIMOTHY 4:12

They say that once you learn to ride a bike,
you never forget. I beg to differ. Okay, so I
haven't really ridden a bike (unless you count the
stationary ones at the YMCA) in about fifteen years.
But last month when we bought our daughters two
new, shiny bikes, I wanted one, too! Suddenly, I had
to have one. So, my husband bought me a beautiful
silver bike—with gearshifts and everything!

I could hardly wait to get home and try it.
The girls thought it was really funny seeing their
old mom on a new bike, but they were supportive
in between giggles. Abby showed me how to use
the gearshifts while Ally reviewed the whole
kickstand thing with me. The bike felt quite foreign
as I shakily began down our driveway. My heart
pounded with fear. It was as if I'd never ridden a

bike in my whole life. Thankfully, my children were there to teach me all of the skills I had forgotten.

You know, we're never too old to learn, and sometimes we neglect to recognize the teachers living in our own homes. Our kids may be younger, but in some ways they are much wiser. Why not let your kids teach you something today?

MOM TO MASTER
Father, help me to never get too old to enjoy my kids. Amen.

WALK ON

That is, that you and I may be
mutually encouraged by each other's faith.
ROMANS 1:12

It was the last day of horse camp, and all of the
parents were on hand to see the campers'
presentation of the skills they'd learned that week.
Smiling proudly, Abby rounded the corner on her
horse. Then, all at once, the old, stubborn horse
stopped. He simply wouldn't budge. Abby ever so
gently kicked the horse in the ribs. Still, the horse
wouldn't go. Then Abby whispered, "Walk on,
Prissy. Walk on." Finally, the horse started moving
forward. Every time the stubborn animal stopped,
Abby would simply say, "Walk on," and the horse
would begin moving again.

As I watched Abby maneuver that large
animal around the ring, I learned something—
encouragement is vitally important. Each time
our kids start to get off that straight and narrow
path, we should softly whisper, "Walk on."
By encouraging our children, we can give them
the confidence to move toward their dreams,

to conquer their fears, and to fulfill the destiny that God has for each of them. Sometimes all they need is a little nudge and a soft, encouraging word to move forward.

Sure, offering encouragement takes time, but it'll be time well spent. So, why not look for opportunities to whisper "Walk on" today? Like Abby's horse, your children will respond positively.

MOM TO MASTER

Father, help me to ever so gently encourage my children. Amen.

PRECIOUS PRAYER TIME

But when you pray, go into
your room, close the door and pray to
your Father, who is unseen.
MATTHEW 6:6

Do you have a sort of bedtime ritual with your children? Some parents read a storybook to their children every night. Other parents share a Bible story or two. Some even make up their own stories to share. Whatever your bedtime routine might be, I hope that prayer is part of it.

Saying a bedtime prayer with your children is one of the most important things you can do for them. It accomplishes several things, such as teaching your kids to pray by hearing you pray aloud, giving prayer a place of importance in their lives, making prayer a habit for them, drawing the family unit closer, and enriching their spiritual side. To put it in the words of my daughter Allyson, "PRAYER ROCKS!"

We spend so much time just doing "stuff" with our kids—running them to soccer practice, helping with homework, playing board games—

and all of that is good. But if we don't figure prayer time into the daily equation, we're just spinning our wheels. Prayer time is a precious time. Don't miss out on it even one night. It's a habit worth forming!

MOM TO MASTER
Father, help me to teach my children the importance of prayer time. Amen.

TOO BUSY TO ENJOY

"If it is the Lord's will,
we will live and do this or that."
JAMES 4:15

I zipped past my father carrying an armload of
dirty laundry. A few seconds later, I zipped past
with a basket of clean laundry. Ten minutes later
I was wrapping Allyson's birthday presents while
talking on the phone. As soon as I put down the
receiver, my father sighed.

"You are too busy, honey," he said, sitting in
the La-Z-Boy chair, watching *The Price Is Right.*

I realized that I had totally ignored my
precious visitor while trying to accomplish the
tasks on my to-do list that morning. My seventy-
nine-year-old dad had just wanted me to sit down
and spend some quality time with him and Bob
Barker. So, I did. I let the answering machine get
the rest of my calls, and I watched TV alongside
my dad, making conversation on commercial

breaks. Dad has suffered several strokes over the past three years, so every moment we have with him is a precious one.

There are times when those to-do lists serve us well, and there are other times when we need to crumple them up and toss them into the trash. That morning taught me something—don't be too busy with life to enjoy life. It's all about prioritizing, really.

MOM TO MASTER

Lord, help me to prioritize my day in a way that is pleasing to You. Amen.

Aiming for Perfection

Aim for perfection, listen to my appeal,
be of one mind, live in peace.
And the God of love and peace will be with you.

2 Corinthians 13:11

Dictionary.com defines perfection like this:

> *perfection (pər-fek-shən) n. The quality*
> *or condition of being perfect. The act or*
> *process of perfecting. A person or thing*
> *considered to be perfect. An instance of*
> *excellence.*

Wow. If I am supposed to be "excellent" all the time, I'm in a heap of trouble. There are some days when I might earn that "Blue Ribbon of Excellence," but there are a lot of days when I wouldn't even qualify for an honorable mention. How about you?

That's why I like the Christian definition of perfection a lot better. One inspirational author defines "Christian perfection" like this: "loving God with all our heart, mind, soul, and strength."

Now that seems more doable to me. In other words, I don't always have to "get it right," but if my heart is right and if I'm truly seeking God, I can walk in Christian perfection. And guess what? You can, too! We may never win another blue ribbon the rest of our lives, but we can still be winners. Who says nobody's perfect? If we're in love with God, we are!

MOM TO MASTER
Father, help me to attain Christian perfection every day of my life. Amen.

THE MYTH OF PERFECTION

You need to persevere so that when
you have done the will of God,
you will receive what he has promised.

HEBREWS 10:36

Taebo. Pilates. Curves. Yep, I've tried them all
(and I'm still trying most of them) to achieve
that perfect body. You know—the bodies we had
before pregnancy? I look at pictures of myself

from my early twenties, and I'm amazed. You could actually see my abdominal muscles! Those were the days. . . .

But, being a determined woman in my mid-thirties, I decided to regain my youthful figure. So, I started exercising more than usual. I traded in my nightly power walk for an intense hour-long Winsor Pilates workout. Once I was able to walk again, I added a thirty-minute resistance workout to my weekly routine. This has been going on for the past three months. Let me just share that I hurt myself in places I didn't even know existed! But I am making progress. And I've learned some things along the way.

Striving for perfection is a painful process no matter if you're trying to achieve the perfect body or the perfect walk with God. Perfection is a myth, really. We are made perfect through Christ Jesus—not through working it as hard as we can. If we keep our eyes on Jesus, He will cause us to succeed.

MOM TO MASTER
Father, help me not to get overwhelmed with the desire to be perfect. I want You to perfect me. Amen.

An Ongoing Project

For we are God's workmanship,
created in Christ Jesus to do good works,
which God prepared in advance for us to do.
Ephesians 2:10

I've always loved this Scripture. Did you know that the word *workmanship* indicates an ongoing process? So, if we are God's workmanship, we are God's ongoing project. In other words, He isn't finished with us yet! Isn't that good news? I am so glad! I'd hate to think that I was as good as I was going to get.

So, if you are feeling less than adequate today, thinking that you are a terrible mother and wife and Christian—cheer up! God is not through with you yet! In fact, He is working on you right now—even as you're reading this devotional. He knew that we'd all make big mistakes, but this Scripture says that He created us in Christ Jesus to do good works. He's prepared the road for us. He's been planning our steps long before we arrived here, so don't worry!

We may not be where we want to be today, but as long as we're farther along than we were yesterday, we're making progress. We're on the right road. After all, we're God's workmanship, and He only turns out good stuff!

MOM TO MASTER
Thank You, God, for working on me, perfecting me from glory to glory. Amen.

NEGATIVE SEEDS

So also, the tongue is a small thing,
but what enormous damage it can do.
JAMES 3:5 NLT

I'm fat!" Abby said, stepping off the
bathroom scales.

"Wonder where she's heard that before?"
Jeff asked, raising his eyebrows at me.

Yes, I've been known to be a slave to the scales.
And, yes, Abby has heard me say that before.
Well, I'm not fat, and neither is she. But, it seemed
that my negative body image had been passed down
to my ten-year-old daughter. With bulimia and
anorexia affecting so many girls and women today,
I realized the seriousness of Abby's statement.

I took Abby's face in my hands, and I said,
"You are not fat. You are the perfect size,
and even if you weren't, that wouldn't change
how special you are to me, your daddy, and your
heavenly Father."

She smiled and took off to play with her sister.

Our words are powerful. They have an effect—
either good or bad. That encounter with Abby

made me reevaluate my words. I repented, and I asked God to uproot those negative seeds that I'd unintentionally planted into Abby's heart and mind. Then I thanked God for His love and for His protection of my children.

If your mouth has been spewing words that aren't uplifting or godly, ask God to uproot those bad seeds. He knows our hearts, and He is a merciful God.

MOM TO MASTER
Thank You, God, for protecting my children from wrong thinking. Amen.

CELEBRATE YOURSELF

A heart at peace gives life to the body.
PROVERBS 14:30

Are you at peace with the person God made
you to be?

If you don't have peace within yourself,
you'll never have peace with other people.
God could send you another mom to be the friend
you've been praying for, but if you're not at peace
with yourself, that relationship won't work.
You've got to be happy with who God made you
to be first before you can experience healthy
relationships.

If you're focused on your imperfections and
are constantly wishing you were someone else,
you're allowing the devil to steal your peace and
replace it with wrong thinking. Don't get caught
in that trap. That's a miserable way to live. Learn
to celebrate the person that God made you to be.

The devil will try to convince you that you're
a weak worm of the dust. He'll try to get you
thinking wrong about yourself. But you need to

declare out loud, "I am a child of the Most High King, and He thinks I'm great."

You may not be happy with every aspect of yourself, but you need to be happy about the basic person that God created you to be. When you start practicing that mindset, your peace will return. And that's a great way to live!

MOM TO MASTER

Lord, I pray that Your peace overtakes me today. Change my wrong thinking. Amen.

THE SELF-PITY PIT

Finally, brothers, whatever is true,
whatever is noble, whatever is right,
whatever is pure, whatever is lovely,
whatever is admirable—if anything is excellent
or praiseworthy—think about such things.
PHILIPPIANS 4:8

Don't go there, girlfriend!"
I have a friend who always says that to me when I am heading toward the self-pity pit. Funny as that expression sounds, it packs a lot of wisdom. If we can stop ourselves before we start wallowing in that self-pity pit, we'll be a lot better off in the long run. See, once you get down in that pit, it's hard to claw your way back out.

For me, all it takes is dwelling on something negative for a few minutes. I'll start to think about the fight I had with my daughters that morning, and the next thing I know, I am looking up from the center of that yucky pit.

I believe that's why the Bible tells us to think on good and lovely things. God knew that if we thought on the other stuff for very long we'd wind up in that old, yucky pit. So, if you're in that pit today, reach up! God is reaching out to you, ready to help you out. Think on Him—not your past failures.

MOM TO MASTER
Lord, help me to spend time thinking on good and lovely things—not my past failures. Amen.

DRIVING OUT FEAR

There is no fear in love.
But perfect love drives out fear.

1 JOHN 4:18

Okay, so I've accepted the fact that I'll never be perfect. But it's good to know that God's perfect love is available to me and that His love drives out fear. You know, as moms, we encounter a lot of fears concerning our children. We fear they won't develop properly when they are growing inside of us. We fear we'll do something wrong as parents. We fear they aren't learning like other children. We fear we aren't spending enough time with them. . .and on and on and on.

But Romans 8:15 tells us that we did not receive a spirit that makes us slaves to fear; rather, we received the Spirit of sonship. That entitles us to the right to cry out to God as our Abba, Father. He wants us to run to Him when we're fearful. He wants to cast that fear right out of our hearts.

So, if you're struggling with fears of inadequacy, or if you're worried about your children to the point that your stomach is in knots—run to God! Let Him replace your fear with His perfect love. Now that's a deal you can't refuse!

MOM TO MASTER
Father, thank You for Your perfect love.
I will not fear because You are my God. Amen.

WHAT A FRIEND

A man of many companions may come to ruin,
but there is a friend who sticks closer than a brother.

PROVERBS 18:24

Sometimes being a mom is a lonely gig. Before my children were born, I was quite the social butterfly, fluttering my way to social event after social event. After Abby and Ally came along, I was lucky to get a shower by noon. So I lost contact with a lot of those social friends—the ones you only see at events. And even some of my dearest buddies from college sort of ditched me once I was a mom. After all, they were still single and living a totally different life. That left me with a few mommy friends I'd met through my MOPS (Mothers of Preschoolers) group and our church. I wasn't very close to any of them, and there wasn't much time for building close relationships

with two toddlers in the house. So, I cried out to God for a friend. That's when I heard that still, small voice say, "I'm your Friend."

Wow. I'd totally forgotten that I had a friend in Jesus—even though I'd sung that hymn a thousand times in my life. So, if you're feeling isolated and friendless today—look up. You've got a friend in Him. I'm thankful for His friendship today.

MOM TO MASTER
Lord, thank You for being my best Friend. Amen.

A Thankful Heart

That my heart may sing
to you and not be silent.
O LORD my God,
I will give you thanks forever.

PSALM 30:12

We teach our kids to say "please and thank you," and that's a good thing. Manners are very important; however, I often wonder if we're just teaching our kids to "go through the motions"

without the proper motivation. In other words, do they just say "thank you" because they know they're supposed to, or are they really thankful?

If I do nothing else right, I want to raise my girls to be thankful, appreciative children. Of course, I'd like them to truly mean their "thank you" responses in day-to-day life. But more than anything, I want them to be thankful to our Lord Jesus Christ for His many blessings.

I think the best way to teach our kids to have thankful hearts toward our heavenly Father is by example. If they see us—their moms—praising God and acknowledging His goodness in everyday life, they'll follow our lead. So, take time to not only teach the manner part of "thank you," but also teach the heart part of "thank you." Let's enter His gates with thanksgiving in our hearts every day! He is worthy of our praise, and our children need to know that. So go on, get your praise on!

MOM TO MASTER
Lord, thank You for being my heavenly Father.
I praise You today! Amen.

My Father's Favorite

You are my God,
and I will give you thanks;
you are my God,
and I will exalt you.

PSALM 118:28

When I think about my earthly father, I always smile. My dad is the kind of dad who dotes on his children. My sister teases that she's his favorite, and I tease back that I am, but in all honesty, he makes both of us feel like the favorite child. And if you asked my brother, he'd say *he* was Dad's favorite! That's just how my dad is, and that's exactly how God is, too. He is a doting Dad. He loves us so much. In fact, He adores us!

But I don't love my dad because he is good to me or even because he makes me feel like I'm his favorite. I love my dad simply because he is Dad. You know, we should love our heavenly Father for that very same reason—not for what He can give us or do for us—but simply because He is our Father. That's what Psalm 118:28 says to me: "You are my God, and I will give you thanks." Tell Him today how much you love Him—just for being Him.

MOM TO MASTER

Father, I want to praise You today just for being You. I am so thankful that You are my heavenly Father. Amen.

GRACE AND MERCY

Always [give] thanks to God
the Father for everything.
EPHESIANS 5:20

She was one of Abby's friends, but this little girl bugged me. I love kids. I even write children's books! But she was a challenge. One afternoon I took Abby and her little friend shopping. While in the Bible bookstore, I purchased a cute cross bracelet for each of them. Abby hugged and thanked me. But the little friend didn't even say thanks! She just slipped on the bracelet and went on her merry way.

I kept thinking, "If she were my daughter, I would be disciplining her right now." But you know what? It wasn't my place to discipline her. My job was simply to show her the love of Jesus. See, God expects us to show grace and mercy to others the same way that He shows grace and mercy to us. And I know there have been times when God has sent down a blessing, and I've "slipped it on" and gone on my merry way. How about you? If you've been less than grateful lately, repent and spend some time thanking God for His goodness today.

MOM TO MASTER

Father, help me to always have a grateful spirit.
Help me to be an example for You. Amen.

Today as Your Last

Why, you do not even know what will happen tomorrow.
What is your life? You are a mist that
appears for a little while and then vanishes.

James 4:14

Not long ago, our pastor posed this question to us: "If you were told you only had a week left to live, what would you do?"

Wow. I hadn't ever thought about that before. Of course, I'd want to spend every second with my family, giving them love and hugs. I wouldn't let the daily stresses of life get to me. I'd focus on the positives. And I think I'd spend a lot of time thanking the people in my life for the love they've always shown me. I'd want them to know how much their love had meant in my life before I headed to heaven.

As I was contemplating these things, our pastor said, "So, why wait? Go ahead and do those things now. You don't need a negative diagnosis to act on those things, do you?"

Well, I guess not. My pastor was right. We can show our love, give hugs, and display our gratitude today. We don't have to wait for a terrible health crisis to shake us up. So, go ahead. Live today like it's your last, because someday it will be.

MOM TO MASTER

Father, I want to thank You for another day of life. I love You. Amen.

MOTIVATION IS KEY

We were not looking for praise from men,
not from you or anyone else.

1 THESSALONIANS 2:6

In fiction writing, your characters always have to have a motivation for their actions. If your reader doesn't understand that motivation, the characters' actions seem contrived and unnatural. Motivation is key.

In life, motivation is key, too. I found this out the hard way. You see, I have always been a people pleaser. I'm the one who will volunteer to bake seventeen pies for the annual bake sale, simply because I want the PTA members to like me and think I'm a really devoted mother. Maybe you're a people pleaser, too.

Being a people pleaser is not only exhausting but also very pointless. First of all, you'll never be able to please everyone. And secondly, if you're doing things for people just to gain their adoration and approval, your motivation is wrong.

Think of it like this—would you still be serving in that way if you weren't going to be recognized or appreciated for your actions? If your answer is yes, then your motivation is right. But if you are doing things simply to gain praise, your motivation might be off. Even if no one ever recognizes your good deeds, take heart—God knows. He's keeping track. And He thinks you're great!

MOM TO MASTER

Lord, help me to keep my motivation pure when serving You and others. Amen.

PRAISING IN THE DARK

I will proclaim the name of the LORD.
Oh, praise the greatness of our God!

DEUTERONOMY 32:3

Have you ever heard the expression "Praise and be raised, or complain and remain"? Now that's a phrase that really packs a punch! It means if you complain about your current circumstances, you'll remain there a lot longer than if you'd just praise the Lord in spite of it all.

Sure, that's easy to say, but it's not so easy to do. I don't know about you, but praising God during difficult times is the last thing I want to do. I'd rather retreat to my bedroom with a box of Junior Mints and sulk awhile. But sulking won't change things any more than complaining will.

By praising God during the dark times, we're telling God that we trust Him—even though we can't see the daylight. Anyone can trust God and praise Him on the mountaintop, but only those who really know God's faithfulness can praise Him in the valley. And it's during those valley times that we truly feel God's tender mercy and experience extreme spiritual growth. So, praise God today—even if you don't feel like it. Through your praise, you open the door for God to work in your life.

MOM TO MASTER

Lord, I praise You in spite of the difficulties in my life. Help me to resist complaining and praise You instead. Amen.

DREAM ON

I can do everything through him
who gives me strength.
PHILIPPIANS 4:13

For a long time, I didn't think it was okay to
have other dreams besides being a mom.
I thought it was selfish to want more. But those
thoughts were not right thinking. I discovered that
God had placed those dreams and desires inside of
me. He is the One who caused me to dream in the
first place, so why should I feel guilty?

Maybe you've always desired to write children's
books, but you thought it was just a crazy whim. If
you're passionate about it—if writing books for
children burns in your heart—it's more than a
whim. It's probably part of God's plan for your life.
Ask Him to show you His plan today. He may not
show you all of it (because it would totally
overwhelm you to see the entire plan), but He will

show you enough to take the initial steps toward the fulfillment of your dream. Isn't that exciting?

Being a mom is the greatest gig we'll ever have, but God doesn't want us to limit ourselves. He can use us—even in the midst of motherhood. Nothing is too big for Him, and nothing is impossible with Him. So, dream on and get with it!

MOM TO MASTER

Lord, help me to follow You down the road that leads to my dream. Amen.

KEEP THE VISION

Where there is no vision,
the people perish.
PROVERBS 29:18 KJV

I've seen it happen with people who retire early
in life. They lose their drive. They lose their
vision. They lose their reason for getting up in the
morning. But you don't have to be of retirement
age to lose your vision. I've also seen young

mothers lose their hope and drive. The devil loves to discourage us and steal our hope.

No matter where we are in life—a mother of a newborn or a mom whose last child just graduated high school—we need to have a goal, a dream, a vision. If we don't, the Word says we'll perish. I don't think it means we'll perish physically, but we'll die spiritually. That's why it's so important to find out God's plan. Do you know God's plan for your life?

If not, ask God to show you His vision for your life. Seek His plan, and once you discover it, write it down and keep it before you. Thank Him for that vision every day. Keep the vision close to your heart, and only share that vision with people you can trust. Your vision is something to be treasured and celebrated.

MOM TO MASTER
Lord, help me to never lose my vision or my drive.
I want to move forward with You. Amen.

PEARLS AND PIGS?

"Do not give dogs what is sacred;
do not throw your pearls to pigs.
If you do, they may trample them under their feet,
and then turn and tear you to pieces."

MATTHEW 7:6

Have you ever heard the expression "Don't
cast your pearls before pigs"? My mama
used to give me that advice when I'd share my
dreams with a friend at school, only to be teased.
Today I find myself sharing that same wisdom with
my girls.

You see, not everyone is going to embrace our
dreams and celebrate our victories with us. It's true!
Even your Christian friends may not want to hear
what God has placed in your heart—especially if
it's bigger than the things they have in their hearts.
Unfortunately, the green-eyed monster lives in
some Christians, too.

So, be careful whom you choose to let in your
inner circle. Don't share your dreams with just
anyone. Your dreams are too precious to waste on
the dogs and pigs. Only share your dreams with

your family and close Christian friends—the ones who will be happy for you and celebrate with you. If you don't have anyone like that in your life, pray that God will send you someone you can trust. And remember, you can always trust Him.

MOM TO MASTER

Thank You, Lord, for giving me such precious dreams. Help me to be careful when sharing them with others that I don't confide in the wrong people. Amen.

Fear Is Lethal

For you did not receive a spirit that
makes you a slave again to fear,
but you received the Spirit of sonship.

Romans 8:15

Are you afraid that you won't ever accomplish your dreams? Do you worry that you're not good enough or smart enough or talented enough to do the things that God has placed in your heart? I think we all face those issues of self-doubt and fear. But we can't allow fear to dwell in our lives. Fear is lethal to our joy level. It's lethal to our self-esteem. And it's lethal to our walk with God.

Think of it this way—where fear begins, failure starts. So, if you're allowing fear to rule your mind, you're not allowing yourself the opportunity to succeed. Fear is the opposite of faith, so you can't be in fear and in faith at the same time. You have to choose. So, choose faith!

Stop the fear tape that's playing in your head. Ask God to fill you with so much faith that there won't be room for any fear. Don't let the devil stop God from using you. Don't let the devil stop you from walking in your dreams. This is your time, and his time is up.

Mom to Master

Lord, fill me with faith. I give You my fears. Amen.

Enjoying Today

The fear of the LORD leads to life:
then one rests content, untouched by trouble.

PROVERBS 19:23

Have you ever heard the expression "Be happy where you are on the way to where you're going"? If you're always looking to the future with longing, you'll miss the good stuff going on right now. You have to find the right balance.

My daughters do this from time to time. When they were younger, they'd get so many presents for Christmas that they couldn't enjoy the ones they'd already opened because they were so focused on opening the next gift. They would hardly look at the roller skates they'd just received before they were on to the next package. It wasn't until all of the presents were unwrapped that they could actually enjoy the blessing load they'd been given.

Have you been guilty of that, too? Are you looking for the next present to unwrap instead of enjoying the blessing load all around you? It's easy to do—especially if you're in the diaper, teething, can't-get-back-into-your-prepregnancy-clothes stage. Some days it's hard to find the "gift" in all of it, but look closely. There are gifts all around. Enjoy this wonderful motherhood journey. Don't miss a minute of it. Every moment should be treasured. You have to enjoy today before you'll ever really appreciate tomorrow.

MOM TO MASTER
Lord, help me to enjoy every minute of this journey. Amen.

HE'LL NEVER LEAVE YOU

Cast all your anxiety on him
because he cares for you.

1 PETER 5:7

When my friend had a stillborn baby several years ago, we were all devastated. I remember when I got the call. I was stunned. None of us knew what to say or do. There were no explanations. And there were no words to comfort her. The only comfort for her pain came from the Word—God's Word. The Lord was there for my friend and her family during this horribly painful time, and that's what pulled them through.

Maybe you've lost a child, or maybe your child has run away from home. I can't pretend to know exactly what you're going through, but God knows. Whatever pain you're experiencing, God is there for you. He loves you, and He cares about your loss. He hurts when you hurt. He longs to comfort you. All you have to do is ask.

While I'll never understand why my wonderful friend lost her baby, I've come to understand one essential thing—God is there for us when we're hurting. He will never leave us. So, cast your cares on Him. He really does care for you—more than you'll ever know.

MOM TO MASTER

Lord, I give my hurt and sense of loss to You today. Thank You for being there for me—no matter what. I love You. Amen.

THE SINGLE MOM

"For your Maker is your husband—
the LORD Almighty is his name—
the Holy One of Israel is your Redeemer;
he is called the God of all the earth."

ISAIAH 54:5

I have a very good friend who is a single mother. She is an amazing woman. She works long hours to pay the bills, and she still finds time to read stories to her little girl. She attends most every school event, and she does it all with a smile on her face. I am in awe of my friend.

When I compliment her, she always says the same thing: "You just do what you have to do." And to be honest, there are days when she doesn't know if she can do it all. She worries about paying the bills on time. She wonders if she'll be able to buy her daughter those designer tennis shoes. She gets lonely. But she knows the most important thing—that God said He would be her husband. She has learned to trust Him for everything in her life. That's how I want to be. I'm thankful for my friend, and I'm thankful for all that she is teaching me about trusting the Lord.

MOM TO MASTER

Lord, please take care of all the single moms in the world. Thank You for being there for all of us. Amen.

ENCOURAGE YOURSELF IN GOD

And the people, that is,
the men of Israel,
encouraged themselves.

JUDGES 20:22 NKJV

Do you ever encourage yourself in the Lord?
As moms, we encourage everybody else—
our husbands, our children, our friends,
our extended family, and our neighbors. But we
rarely take time to encourage ourselves. Instead,
we're overly critical of ourselves. We allow the
devil to beat us up, telling us how awful we are.
If we'll listen long enough, the devil will convince
us that we're unworthy to be servants of God.
He'll tell us that we're horrible parents and wives.
He'll tell us that we're failures in life. The devil
will serve us condemnation with a side of guilt as
often as we'll let him. So tell him, "NO MORE!"

We have to stop allowing the devil to deceive
us. Don't dwell on his lies; meditate on God's Word.
The Bible says that you are fully able to fulfill your
destiny. It says that no weapon formed against you
is going to prosper. It says that you can do

everything through God's strength. Stop focusing on what you can't do and start focusing on what you can do. Quit looking at how far you've got to go, and start looking at how far you've already come. Encourage yourself in the Lord today! It's your turn.

MOM TO MASTER
Thank You, Lord, for giving me the ability to fulfill my destiny. Help me to stay encouraged. Amen.

CHASE THE DARK CLOUDS

"Do not sorrow,
for the joy of the LORD
is your strength."
NEHEMIAH 8:10 NKJV

Do you know a person who is a "gloom and doomer"? You know the type—the person who never has a good day. The person you never ask, "How are you?" because you'll be there listening to her misfortunes, bad luck, and illnesses

for hours. Maybe you're a gloom and doom kind of gal. If you are, there's hope.

You don't have to live with a dark cloud over your head anymore. God is your way out of gloom and doom. He will help you make joyful living a way of life.

Determine today to become a positive person—not only for your sake but also for the sake of your kids. They pick up on our defeatist attitudes. They will become mini gloom and doomers if we allow that spirit of hopelessness and depression to invade our homes. So, let's get all of the gloom and doom out of our lives once and for all. Get in the habit of saying these confessions every day: "I am well able to fulfill my destiny. God has made me an overcomer. No weapon formed against me is going to prosper. The joy of the Lord is my strength." Before long, that dark cloud that's been blocking the Son is sure to move out!

MOM TO MASTER
Lord, help me to be a positive person. Amen.

No More Mean Streaks!

For God is working in you,
giving you the desire to obey him
and the power to do what pleases him.
PHILIPPIANS 2:13 NLT

Do you ever feel rebellious? My mother calls
that a "mean streak." It seems my mean
streak is a mile wide at times. Bottom line?
I sometimes have a hard time being obedient.
Maybe you have that same challenge. But here's
the good news: Whether or not you realize it,
God is at work on the inside of you. He is
constantly fixing you so that you'll want to
obey Him. He loves us so much that He is willing
to work on us until our mean streaks are entirely
gone. He will never give up on us! He doesn't
dwell on our disobedience. He sees us through
eyes of love. The more we understand that love,
the more we'll want to walk in obedience.
The more we embrace our Father's love, the more
we'll want to please Him.

Here's more good news: God is doing that
same work on the inside of our children. So, when

they want to disobey, He is willing to go that extra mile to help them *want* to obey. See, He loves our children even more than we do. As we become more obedient to God and His ways, we'll become better examples for our children. It's a win/win situation.

MOM TO MASTER
Heavenly Father, thank You for helping me become more obedient. Amen.

WAIT FOR YOUR MIRACLE

*"But as for me and my family,
we will serve the LORD."*

JOSHUA 24:15 NLT

Are your children serving the Lord? Have they made Jesus the Lord of their lives? If you have a wayward child, I know the heartache you must be experiencing. But remember this: It ain't over until the fat lady sings, and she hasn't even stood up! It may look like your child is rebelling against you and God, but keep praying. Keep believing. Find Scriptures to stand on. Have faith that God is working behind the scenes to bring your child into the Kingdom.

It may look hopeless right now, but God is our hope and glory. He loves your child more than you do. He is able to turn situations around without even getting up from His throne. So, don't worry. Only believe. During this time of praying for your child's salvation, surround yourself with the Word of God. Listen to praise and worship music. Watch Christian TV. Read the Word. Read Christian books. Immerse yourself in God and let Him build your faith.

Remember the story of the prodigal son in Luke 15? I'm sure that father thought he'd lost his son for good. But he hadn't. The son returned. Your child will return, too. Don't give up. Stand your ground and wait for your miracle.

MOM TO MASTER

Lord, thank You for protecting my wayward child. I praise You that my child is coming into the Kingdom. In Jesus' name. Amen.

SHARE GOD WITH OTHERS

And I sought for a man among them,
that should make up the hedge,
and stand in the gap before me for the land,
that I should not destroy it: but I found none.

EZEKIEL 22:30 KJV

We all know that we need God, but have you ever thought that God might need us, too? Sure, He is Almighty God. Still, God needs His people. In fact, He needs people like you and me, working for Him and accomplishing His goals here on earth. More than anything, He is looking for willing hearts to take the message of His Son around the world.

As moms, we can do that in our own neck of the woods. Our world might be our children's ball games, the grocery store, Wal-Mart, the dry cleaners, our workplace, our neighborhood, our children's school. . . We don't have to travel to Africa to evangelize. We can touch the people in our little corner of the world with His love.

Look for opportunities to share God with others. If you're at the grocery store and you notice that your checker is having a hard day, say, "How are you doing today?"

If she says, "Well, I'm not feeling very well," simply ask, "Do you mind if I pray for you? I'd be happy to do that while you're ringing up my items." I've never had anyone say no yet. They are grateful, and God is pleased.

MOM TO MASTER

Lord, help me to touch my world with
Your love. Amen.

USE YOUR WORDS WISELY

But no man can tame the tongue.
It is a restless evil, full of deadly poison.
JAMES 3:8

Words can be lethal weapons. Did you
know that? With our mouths, we can
curse someone and do irreparable damage to that
person. I was watching one of the daytime talk
shows not long ago while I walked on the treadmill, and the title of the show was "You Ruined
My Life." All of the guests who came onto that
show shared heartbreaking stories of how someone had said horrible things to them, changing the
entire course of their lives. Some of these guests
had lived with the sting of these words for more
than twenty years. Can you believe that?

The guests who were the most messed up had
internalized damaging words from their parents.
Wow. That show just put an exclamation mark at

the end of what I already knew in my heart—
we need to speak good things to our children!
We should take every opportunity to tell our kids,
"You can do it! You are well able to fulfill your
destiny! You've got what it takes! No weapon
formed against you is going to prosper! I love you,
and God loves you!" So use your words wisely.
They hold the power of life and death.

MOM TO MASTER
*Lord, help me to speak only good things to my
children. Amen.*

THE BIG "C"

The mouth of the righteous man utters wisdom,
and his tongue speaks what is just.

PSALM 37:30

D o you ever feel like you've got a big C
on your head, indicating your level of
cluelessness? I am sure my C is visible from time
to time. Growing up, I always thought that when
I became a mom, I'd have all the answers. After
all, my mom always had the answers. But I've
discovered being a mom doesn't necessarily come
with the "Answer Key for Life."

Many times I am clueless. Maybe you're
clueless, too. But, thank the Lord, we don't have to
remain clueless. Even if we don't have the answers,
God does. And here's the best part—He is more
than willing to share that wisdom with us so that
we can pass it on to our children.

It's perfectly okay to admit ignorance when
you don't know the answer to a question that your
kiddos come up with—really. Just tell them,

"I don't know, but I'll find out. God has all the answers, and He is willing to share them with me." It's good for our children to see us vulnerable once in a while. It's especially good for them to see us seeking God for His wisdom. So, go ahead, wipe that C off your head and seek God.

MOM TO MASTER
Lord, please fill me with Your wisdom so that I can impart it to my children. Amen.

THREE LITTLE WORDS

Love never fails.

1 CORINTHIANS 13:8

D o you know that some children grow up without ever hearing "I love you" said to them by their parents? It's true. Maybe you're one of the people who grew up without ever hearing those three important words. If you are, then I'm sure you know how hurtful and devastating it is to never feel loved.

I have a friend who grew up in a home like that—where love was never communicated— and she has struggled in that area. Her father used to say, "I don't have to say it. My actions show that I love you." While that might be true, we still need to hear the words. As wives, we need to hear those three words from our husbands. And as moms, we need to communicate our love to our children.

There are many ways we can say "I love you." We can leave little love notes to our spouses and our children, sneaking them into briefcases and backpacks. We can verbally express our love every morning and every night. We can bake a big cookie cake and write "I Love You!" on it. Be as creative as you want, just make sure you take time to express your love every day. Be an ambassador of love in your home.

MOM TO MASTER

Father, help me to better express my love to my family. Amen.

A LOST ART FORM

*"Go near and listen to all that
the LORD our God says."*
DEUTERONOMY 5:27

D o you talk too much? Listening has become
sort of a lost art form in today's society.
We are a generation of people who simply
love to hear ourselves talk. But, you know, if we're

constantly talking, we're missing out on a lot. This is especially true in our prayer lives.

When you pray, do you do all of the talking? From the time we're little children, we're taught to pray to God. We're taught to say the Lord's Prayer. We're taught to bring our praises and petitions unto Him. But very few of us are taught to wait upon the Lord and listen for His voice. It's a difficult thing, waiting and listening. It requires time on our part. It requires patience. It takes practice. God's voice doesn't come down from the sky and speak to us in a Charlton Heston-type voice. No, He speaks to us through that still, small voice—that inward knowing—the Holy Spirit. He also speaks to us through His Word.

So, quit doing all of the talking and take time to listen to Almighty God! He has much wisdom to share with us if we'll only be quiet long enough to receive it.

MOM TO MASTER
Lord, I want to hear Your voice. Help me to listen better. Amen.

You Go, Girl!

*"If you have a message of encouragement
for the people, please speak."*
Acts 13:15

Y ou go, girl!"
That has sort of become the expression
of today's women, hasn't it? In the past, Helen
Reddy's "I am woman, hear me roar" was the cry,
but now it's simply an encouraging "You go, girl!"
We need to encourage each other. As moms, we
should uplift one another in prayer, in word, and
in deed.

I don't know what I would do without the gal
pals in my life. There are days when I need to call
and vent. There are times when I simply need my
buddy to say, "You don't look fat." There are
situations when I just need a hug and a simple
"You go, girl! You can do it!"

As moms, we are constantly speaking words
of encouragement to our families. We're the
cheerleaders! But we need a little cheering every
so often, too. That's why it's so important to
surround yourself with positive people. Find friends

who are women of faith, and be there for
one another. Pray for one another. Love one
another. And encourage each other with a "You go,
girl!" now and then. We're all in this motherhood
experience together, so let's cheer each other on
to victory!

MOM TO MASTER
Lord, thank You for the friends You've given me.
Help me to encourage them as You encourage me.
Amen.

SPEAK FROM YOUR HEART

My heart overflows with a beautiful thought!
I will recite a lovely poem to the king,
for my tongue is like the pen of a skillful poet.
PSALM 45:1 NLT

D o you want your tongue to be like the pen of a skillful poet? That's a lofty goal but one that is totally within our reach if we let God fill our hearts with His love. You see, the Word says that out of the heart the mouth speaks. So, if your heart is full of ugliness and trash, then your tongue will be writing ugly things.

As moms, we need to write very skillfully with our tongues because those "little poets" who call us Mom are taking notes all the time. They listen very carefully to everything we say—good or bad. We only have a short time to impact our kids for the Kingdom of God, so we need to make every word count.

Sure, we're going to miss it sometimes. We're only human. But it should be our goal to be more like Jesus every day. If we become more Christlike, then our mouths will be like the pens of skillful poets, writing good things on the hearts of all we encounter.

MOM TO MASTER

Heavenly Father, help me to use my words wisely. Fill my heart with Your love so that my mouth might be filled with Your words. Amen.

The Wisdom of Women

Timely advice is as lovely as
golden apples in a silver basket.
Proverbs 25:11 NLT

It's funny—as young children we thought our moms knew everything. As teens, we thought they knew nothing. As adults, we realize we were right in the first place—they do know everything. Moms are full of wisdom; however, when I became a mom, I didn't feel so wise. In fact, I didn't know the first thing about being a mother. As I've matured, I've learned a little about being a mom—mostly from my mom. Her advice is priceless.

We can learn much from the godly women in our lives. Maybe your mom hasn't been there for you, but God has placed other women in your life—an aunt, a grandmother, a close family friend, or your pastor's wife. Cherish their words of wisdom. God has placed them in your life for a purpose.

Just think, some day your children will look to you for wisdom—it's true! The Word says that they will rise up and call you blessed. So, make

sure you have some wisdom to share. Treasure
the advice that's been given to you, and more
importantly, meditate on the Word of God.
There's much wisdom waiting for you!

MOM TO MASTER

*Heavenly Father, thank You for those special women
in my life. Help me to honor them and You. Amen.*

Awaken with Praise

In the morning, O LORD, you hear my voice;
in the morning I lay my requests before you
and wait in expectation.

PSALM 5:3

How do you start your mornings? Do you roll out of bed, grumbling and grumpy? Or do you spring out of bed, praising the Lord with great expectation? If you're like me, you're not exactly chipper in the morning. But I'm learning to like those early hours a little better. Why? Because mornings are a great time to praise the Lord!

If you start your day giving praises to God, it's even more energizing than a shot of espresso. No matter how grumpy you feel, once you start praising God for His love and His goodness, you're bound to change your mood for the better. That's just the way it works!

So, why not use your mouth for something worthwhile like praising the Lord? Begin each day thanking God. It will take some practice, but you'll get the hang of it. The Holy Spirit will help you. Praise God for the many blessings in your life. Praise Him for another day to be alive. Praise Him just because He is God and deserving of our praise. Let your children see you praising the Lord, and encourage them to join in. If you do, the mornings around your house will be a lot brighter.

MOM TO MASTER
Lord, I praise You for who You are. Amen.

HONESTY—THE BEST POLICY

"Whoever would love life and see
good days must keep his tongue from
evil and his lips from deceitful speech."

1 PETER 3:10

When I was a little girl, I lied to my father just once. When he found out, I received a few licks across my backside, but that didn't hurt nearly as much as what my dad said to me. He looked me in the eyes and uttered, "There's nothing I dislike more than a lie. I am disappointed in you."

Whoa! I could handle anything except my dad being disappointed in me. Today, as a mom of two little girls, I've been on the other side of that lying scenario a time or two. And I've discovered that I don't like being lied to any more than my father did.

It's not enough to just tell our children that lying is a sin. We need to take every opportunity to let them know that lying always has consequences. Once when I caught the girls in a lie, I told them that even if they got away with their lie, and I never found out about it, God would always know. That got their attention. You see, they love God, and they didn't want to disappoint Him any more than I wanted to disappoint my earthly father. So, strive for honesty in your house. God will be pleased, and that's no lie!

MOM TO MASTER
Lord, help me to raise honest, godly children. Amen.

ACTIONS SPEAK LOUDER

*Dear children, let us not love with words
or tongue but with actions and in truth.*

1 JOHN 3:18

Saying "I love you" to our children is very
important. They need to hear those words on
a daily basis. But we also need to *show* that we love
our children. Have you ever really thought about
the common expression "Actions speak louder than
words"? There's a lot of truth to that saying.

While it's easy to say "I love you," it's not so
easy to show our love all the time. That's why
another expression, "Talk is cheap," is used so
often. As moms, we need to find ways to back up
our "I love yous" every single day. In other words,
walk the talk.

Make a conscious effort today to do something
special for your children—something out of the
ordinary. Leave them little love notes. Make them
a special pancake breakfast and serve it by

candlelight for added fun. Plan a family night out at one of their favorite places. Just find a unique way to show your kids how much you adore them. Ask God to help you in this area. He will. After all, the Bible says that God is love. He is the expert in showing love.

MOM TO MASTER
Heavenly Father, help me to show Your love to my family on a daily basis. I love You. Amen.

Walk with Integrity

*"I know, my God, that you test the heart
and are pleased with integrity."*

1 Chronicles 29:17

My dad often talks about a time when a handshake and a man's word were the only things needed to seal a deal. There was no need for contracts. Everybody operated on trust and integrity. Can you imagine if the world were still

like that today? Giving someone your word should be enough, but integrity—even among Christians—is hard to come by these days. After you've been burned a few times, it's easy to become jaded and start questioning everyone's integrity.

As Christians, and as mothers, we should walk in integrity. Of course, we know it's wrong to lie. That's a given. But there are other ways that we compromise our integrity. For instance, if you tell friends that you'll meet them at 10 a.m. and you don't show up until 10:20, that's a lack of integrity. The Lord convicted me of this just the other day because as anyone who knows me will testify, I am notoriously late.

It's our goal to set good examples for our children, right? So, let's determine today to be people of integrity in every area of our lives. Integrity is important to God, and it should be important to us.

Mom to Master
Lord, mold me into a person of integrity,
and help me to teach my children to walk
in integrity, too. Amen.

STAND YOUR GROUND

The fear of the LORD is
the beginning of knowledge,
but fools despise wisdom and discipline.
PROVERBS 1:7

Nobody likes to hear the word no—
especially our children! We have a rule at
our house that simply states, "No playtime until
your homework is finished." Well. . .that's not
always a popular rule. Maybe you have the same
rule. If you do, I'll bet you occasionally get the
same reaction I do—"Mom! Please! I don't have
that much homework. I can finish it later. Let us
ride our bikes now."

Yes, I have made exceptions to the rule for
special outings and parties, but the rule stands
most of the time. We have to think "future
minded" for our kids because they live in "the
now." I know that if they ride their bikes after
school, they'll come in tired and grouchy and have
no energy left to do their homework. And if they

don't complete their homework, they'll make bad grades. And if they make bad grades, they'll have to be grounded. It's a whole chain reaction of negative circumstances, which is why we came up with the "homework first rule" in the first place.

So, don't be afraid to stand your ground. Don't cave in to the whining and begging. Your rules are for your children's own good—even if they don't see it that way.

MOM TO MASTER

Lord, give me the wisdom to make good rules and the authority to implement them and stick by them. Amen.

THE PARENTING BOOK

A refusal to correct is a refusal to love;
love your children by disciplining them.

PROVERBS 13:24 MSG

Have you ever spent any time with children
who have never been disciplined? You know
the kind—the ones who run all over a restaurant,
scream when they don't get their way, and show
disrespect to everyone. We spent some time with
one of these children not long ago. This little girl
was unbelievable! She broke toys. She intentionally
hurt animals. She backtalked to her parents.
And she disobeyed every direction. I desperately
wanted to discipline her, but it wasn't my place.
It was her parents' place. Unfortunately, the parents
didn't believe in discipline. They apparently read
some book about allowing a child to develop his or
her own boundaries.

The only parenting book that's truly needed is
God's Word. Proverbs 13:24 tells us that we show
love by disciplining our children. In fact, that

verse clearly states that it is actually a refusal to love if we don't correct our children. So, while Junior may not feel loved at the exact moment he is being punished, he is experiencing love.

Don't be fooled by the world's way of doing things. God's way is always the better choice. He knows a thing or two about parenting. After all, He is a parent. So, ask Him for wisdom and guidance when it comes to disciplining your children. He has all the answers.

Mom to Master

Lord, teach me to be a better parent. Amen.

GO TO THE SOURCE

The rod of correction imparts wisdom,
but a child left to himself disgraces his mother.
PROVERBS 29:15

No matter where you stand on the spanking issue, this verse holds good meaning. You see, it's not so much about the spanking, it's about the wisdom that we impart when we discipline our children.

There are lots of differing opinions about how to discipline our children. Some experts say we should spank them with our hands. Others say we should spank, but only with a paddle. Still others say we should never spank, only punish by other means. It seems there is a new theory every year. So, what is the answer?

God is the only true answer. You must seek His face and ask His direction. He will teach you how to discipline your kids. He loves them even more than you do. He won't lead you astray. Just trust Him. Don't get caught up asking lots of people how you should discipline your kids. If you ask a hundred people, you'll get a hundred different perspectives. They don't know any more than you do. Go to the Source. He will impart wisdom to you so that you can impart wisdom to your children. You see, discipline and wisdom go hand in hand.

MOM TO MASTER
Lord, teach me the best way to discipline my children. Amen.

The Popular Mom

A fool spurns his father's discipline,
but whoever heeds correction shows prudence.

PROVERBS 15:5

Did you know that parenting isn't a popularity contest? If it were, I would've lost a long time ago. How about you? No, as moms we have to make some decisions that aren't very popular at times. We have to tell our children they can't go see some of the popular movies, even though all of their friends are going. We have to forbid them from attending certain parties, even though they don't understand why. It's all a part of what we do as moms.

It's the heartbreaking part of our job. I don't like having to say no to my girls. I want them to have fun. I want them to experience life. I want them to enjoy as much as possible. But I also want to protect them and nurture them and teach them in the ways of the Lord. And sometimes those wants contradict one another.

Yes, I want my kids to think I'm cool.
Yes, I want them to think of me as a friend.
But more than anything else, I want to raise my
girls to love God and walk in His ways. If that
means making some unpopular decisions, then
that's okay by me. God still thinks we're special.
We'll always be popular to God.

MOM TO MASTER
*Lord, help me to stand my ground even when it's not
the popular thing to do. Amen.*

Too Many Choices!

If you are guided by the Spirit,
you won't obey your selfish desires.
GALATIANS 5:16 CEV

Did you know that we make approximately twenty-five hundred choices every single day of our lives? (No wonder I'm so exhausted at the end of the day!) So, if you aren't happy with your current life, you're probably making lousy decisions. The only way to make good, solid decisions is to turn off your reasoning mechanism and allow the Holy Spirit to guide you. Discernment and reasoning can't operate at the same time. Our minds reason, but our spirits discern. I don't know about you, but I don't trust my mind. I'd much rather rely on the leading of the Holy Spirit to make decisions—especially when it comes to disciplining my children.

With so many conflicting opinions in the media, I get easily confused. I don't want to be a tyrant, but I don't want to be a wimp, either.

I want to raise good, godly kids, but I don't want to shove the Word down their throats.

There are no easy answers. What works for one parent/child relationship might not work for another. So, don't reason and worry your life away. Instead, ask for God's leading to help you make the best possible decisions. He will help you in the area of disciplining your kids. He has all of the answers.

MOM TO MASTER

Lord, I am asking for Your leading today. Help me to do things Your way. Amen.

TEN LESSONS

Come, children, listen closely;
I'll give you a lesson in GOD worship.
PSALM 34:11 MSG

If you could teach your children only ten things before you died, what would you share? Would you teach them to stand up for who they are in Christ Jesus? Would you teach them self-defense? Would you teach them good manners? Would you teach them to give to others? Would you teach them to treat others with respect? Would you teach them how to be a friend?

It's a tough call, isn't it? There are so many things we want to impart to our kids. We want to save them from making all of the stupid mistakes that we made. While we can't protect them from every mistake, we can put them on the road to success and happiness.

We can make the most of every opportunity to teach them about the nature of God—God the Healer, God the Provider, God the Savior,

God the Deliverer, God the Great I Am! There are
chances every day to share little lessons with our
children. Ask the Lord to help you identify those
opportunities so that you can take advantage of
each one.

MOM TO MASTER

*Lord, help me to share Your love with my children
each day. And, Lord, help me to take advantage of
every opportunity to teach my kids about You. Amen.*

LOVING TOO MUCH

He will die for lack of discipline,
led astray by his own great folly.

PROVERBS 5:23

Obviously, this verse in Proverbs lets us know that discipline is an important part of our job as parents. No, it's not fun. No, it's not popular. But it is very necessary. In fact, it's so necessary that if we don't correct our children and

bring them up in the way of the Lord, they are sure to suffer.

None of us would intentionally hurt our kids. We love them. But sometimes we love them too much, meaning we don't discipline them for their wrong behavior. We let them get away with wrongdoing simply because we don't want to hurt their feelings or make a scene in front of their friends. But if we don't teach them right from wrong, they won't know how to make godly decisions. They'll make wrong choices, which will lead to heartache, ruin, and, ultimately, destruction.

Our role is crucial. Ask the Lord to help you be firm yet loving as you discipline your kids. Ask Him for wisdom. You can do it. God has equipped you with everything you need to be a good parent.

Mom to Master
Lord, I need Your divine intervention—help me to discipline my children so that they will follow You all the days of their lives. Amen.

Miracles for the Future

So do not throw away your confidence;
it will be richly rewarded.

Hebrews 10:35

Are you focusing on the future, or are you having trouble seeing past the endless piles of dirty laundry that are in front of you right now? When today has so many worries, responsibilities, and obligations, it's difficult to be future minded. But we need to make a conscious effort. We need to let God stir up our faith. We need to start believing God for big things. We need to realize that even if the circumstances aren't so great today, God is bringing about a miracle in our future.

You see, no matter what you're dealing with today, God has a plan that will work things out better than you could ever imagine—if you'll just get your faith eyes in focus and become future minded. Ask God to help you change your focus.

The enemy doesn't want you to stand in faith for the fulfillment of your destiny. He doesn't

want to see your children walking with God.
He wants you to worry about all of the problems
of today and forget about your future. Don't fall
for the devil's plan. Focus on the future. See your
children well and serving God. See your family
happy and whole. See your dirty laundry washed,
folded, and put away. Get a vision of victory today!

MOM TO MASTER

*Lord, help me get my faith eyes in focus and looking
toward the future. Amen.*

The Owner's Manual

Therefore put on the full armor of God,
so that when the day of evil comes,
you may be able to stand your ground,
and after you have done everything, to stand.

Ephesians 6:13

We all face challenges in life. Some days we face more challenges than others. Let's face it, being a parent is a tough job. When you have children, there's no manual that comes with the job. Sure, there are lots of parenting books and magazines, but they all say conflicting things, giving opposing advice.

There's only one manual that covers it all. From disciplining your children to showing them unconditional love, the Word of God has got you covered. Need an answer for a specific situation? Don't rely on secondhand information. Go to the Source. Read the Word and let it come alive to you.

Stand strong as you face challenges. Don't bow down to them. Remain faithful. Fight that good fight of faith. Keep feeding on the Word and standing firm. If you'll stay in faith, God will promote you. He loves to bless His children. Make yourself a good candidate for His supernatural blessing flow. Keep standing. I don't care how bad it might look right now, stand strong. Go to the Manual. Your answers and your promotion are on the way. Hallelujah!

MOM TO MASTER

Father, help me to stand strong in the face of difficulty. I love You. Amen.

LIVING TO GIVE

"Give, and it will be given to you:
good measure, pressed down,
shaken together, and running over."

LUKE 6:38 NKJV

Did you know that God wants you to be
happy? He desires for you to live life to its
fullest. It doesn't matter that you might be elbow
deep in diapers and carpools right now—you can
still enjoy life!

One of the main ways you can guarantee joy in
your life is by living to give. You see, true happiness
comes when we give of ourselves to others—
our spouses, our children, our extended family,
our church, our community, and our friends.
As moms, we're sort of trained to be givers.
We give up our careers, many times, to become
full-time moms. We give up a full night's sleep to
feed our babies. We give up sports cars for
minivans and SUVs to accommodate our families.
In fact, we'd give our lives for our children.

But sometimes our attitudes are less than
joyful in all of our giving, right? Well, rejoice

today. God promises to multiply back to you everything that you give. When you step out in faith, you open a door for God to move on your behalf. It's the simple principle of sowing and reaping. And as mothers, we are super sowers. So, get ready for a super huge harvest!

MOM TO MASTER
Lord, help me to live to give with the right attitude. I love You. Amen.

THE BEST CARETAKER

"Now I am giving him to the LORD,
and he will belong to the LORD his whole life."

1 SAMUEL 1:28 NLT

Have you truly given your children to God?
Sure, we all say those words when our
babies go through the dedication service at
church, but how many of us truly mean them?
It's so easy to take back our kids. We trust God
with everything in our lives, but when it comes to
our children, we want to take care of them.
We love them so much that we are afraid to give
them to God. What if He calls them into the
mission field in some unstable or war-torn country?
What if He asks them to move across the country
to begin a church? What if *His* plans for your child
conflict with your dreams for your baby?

It's scary, isn't it? But it shouldn't be. As moms,
we have to realize that God loves our children

even more than we do. If He calls them into a war-torn country to serve Him, then that will be the place that holds happiness and peace for them. After all, being in the center of God's will is the safest place a person can be. So, don't worry. Giving your kids to God is the best thing you can do for them.

MOM TO MASTER
Lord, I give my children to You today. Amen.

A Supernatural Peace

*"'The LORD turn his face toward you
and give you peace.'"*

Numbers 6:26

Have you ever asked the Lord to give you peace? I don't think that's one of those things we typically ask for as moms. But peace is available to us.

I'm not talking about that kind of temporal peace that a nice, long, hot bath brings. (Although, I'm not opposed to that, either!) I'm talking about the kind of peace that only the Father can give— the kind of peace that is present even in the midst of chaos. The Bible says it's a peace that surpasses all understanding. In other words, it's a kind of peace that people don't understand. It's hard to put into words.

I once interviewed a man and wife who understood this kind of peace. After having a premature baby who required three major surgeries during her first year of life, they got pregnant again. And again, the baby came early. This time the little baby only lived five and a half months. I asked them how they made it through that time, and they both said, "We had a supernatural peace." That's the kind of peace that I want to walk in every day— how about you? Let's ask God for it today.

MOM TO MASTER
Lord, please give me Your supernatural peace today, and help me to walk in that peace every day. Amen.

FEED YOUR FAITH

For everyone born of God overcomes the world.
This is the victory that has
overcome the world, even our faith.

1 JOHN 5:4

A re you feeling discouraged today? Are you
about ready to throw in the towel? Have
you given motherhood all that you've got, and you
still don't feel like you're winning the race?
We've all been there. And when I start feeling like
that, I used to grab a Diet Coke and a chocolate
bar and comfort myself. I'd dwell in the land of
"Poor Pitiful Pearl" for a while before I'd ever go
to God. Somehow, feeding my face with chocolate
made me feel better. (It cost me more miles on
the treadmill, though.) But now I've learned that
feeding my faith works much better to pull me out
of discouragement than feeding my face!

The Bible says that faith comes by hearing the
Word of God. As you hear the Word and store it
in your heart, your faith grows stronger. So, listen

to the Bible on tape while you do your housework
or while you're on the treadmill. Then the next
time the enemy tries to make you feel worthless,
discouraged, depressed, worried, or overwhelmed,
you can put your faith to work by declaring the
Word of God. Feed your faith, not your face.
You'll feel much better!

MOM TO MASTER
*Lord, I am feeling discouraged today. Please fill me
up with more of You. Amen.*

FILL 'ER UP

I will refuse to look at anything vile and vulgar.
Psalm 101:3 NLT

Have you ever heard a preacher say, "Give the devil no place in your life!" I always thought that was kind of an odd statement, because I would never give the devil a place in my life. But as it turns out, I was giving the devil a place in my life simply by allowing him in my thought life.

Did you know that what you think determines the direction and quality of your life? That's why the Bible tells us to think on things that are pure and lovely in Philippians 4:8. But in order to think on those things, we need to monitor what we allow into our hearts. That means we need to be careful about what we watch, read, and listen to. We need to fill our thoughts with the promises of God—promises of joy, peace, freedom, prosperity, and more!

We also need to monitor what we give our children to watch, read, and listen to. While spending the night at a friend's house, Abby recently saw a movie that she shouldn't have seen. Then she suffered with nightmares for weeks! Don't let fear and other negative material get into your children's hearts and minds. Be that filter for them. As a family, think on lovely things and give the devil no place in your home.

MOM TO MASTER
Lord, help me to feed on Your Word and only think on lovely things. Amen.

There's Always Hope

"There's hope for your children."
GOD's Decree.

Jeremiah 31:17 msg

Are your children away from God right now? Are they in a state of rebellion? If they are, I know that you're heartbroken. And even if you're not in this situation, I bet you know someone who is. It's tough. When we've raised our children to know the things of God and they still rebel, we immediately start blaming ourselves. We wonder where we went wrong. We wonder what we could have done differently. Well, stop wondering and start praising the Lord!

You may not feel like praising the Lord right now, but that's exactly what you must do. You see, the Word says that your children will return to the Lord. The Word says there is hope for your children. The Word says that if you have the faith of a mustard seed, you can move mountains.

So, hey, bringing your children back to God is no biggie! God can do that in the twinkling of an eye!

But you must praise God for the victory even before it takes place. He has commanded that we live in victory, so that means no matter how bad it looks right now, you can be encouraged. We already know how it ends—we win! We walk in victory, side by side with our children. Praise the Lord today! Your victory is on its way!

MOM TO MASTER

Lord, I praise You for my children's salvation. Amen.

You're Covered

So we say with confidence,
"The Lord is my helper;
I will not be afraid."

HEBREWS 13:6

What's on your agenda today? Are you facing some big challenges? No matter what you're going to be up against today, God's got you covered. He says in Hebrews that He will be our helper. We don't have to be afraid.

I don't know about you, but I sometimes feel afraid. Sure, I put on a good outward appearance, but on the inside I feel insecure. I wonder if I'm doing a good enough job as a mom. Do you ever wonder if you're measuring up? I especially feel that way when I am around moms who are doing everything right. You know, the really cool mom who has a clean house, all of her laundry folded and put away, no dirty dishes in the sink ever, well-mannered children, and a perfect figure, too! I want to be a mom like that someday.

But until then, I am declaring that "I will not be afraid." God did not give us a spirit of fear, but of love and of power and of a sound mind. We are up to any challenge. We can do all things through Him. We can be confident in Him today and every day.

MOM TO MASTER
Thank You, Lord, for helping me every single day of the year. I couldn't do it without You. I love You, God. Amen.

GOD KNOWS YOUR HEART

*"Your Father knows exactly what you need
even before you ask him!"*
MATTHEW 6:8 NLT

Have you ever been so distraught that you
didn't even know what to pray? I think
we've all been there at some point in our lives.
After my father had his first stroke and they didn't
know if he would live through the night, I became
numb. It was touch and go for several days, and all
I did was drive to and from the hospital. On those
forty-minute drives, I would try to pray, but all I
could do was say the name of Jesus. Thankfully,
that was enough.

In Matthew 6:8, the Word tells us that God
knows what we need even before we ask Him.
That's good to know, isn't it? Even when we can't
pray what we want to pray, God knows our hearts.
He knows what we need. If we simply call on the
name of Jesus, He is right there beside us.

No matter how desperate you are today. No matter how hopeless you feel. No matter how far from God you think you are. . .God loves you. He wants to help you. He wants to help your children. He wants to bring you through this difficult time. Call on Him today.

MOM TO MASTER

Thank You, Lord, for knowing me so well and hearing my heart. Amen.

Get Out of the Rut

O God, let me sing a new song to you.
Psalm 144:9 msg

Is your prayer life in a rut? Do you pray the same words over and over, day after day, month after month, and year after year? If so, you're in a prayer rut. And the only way out of a prayer rut is to sing a new song. Praise the Lord with a new song, as it says in Psalm 144. Don't just ask God to bless everyone from your husband to your pet fish, Bubbles. Instead, spend some time just worshipping the Lord. Tell Him you love Him because He gave you wonderful children. Tell Him you adore Him for putting a roof over your head. Praise Him for the food He gives each day. Most of all, praise Him because He died on a cross so that you might live.

God is a good God. He is worthy of our praise. If you have trouble thinking of things to praise Him for during your prayer time, use the Bible to help. Quote Scriptures such as, "You are worthy of my praise, for Your mercy and goodness endure forever." Praise Him from the bottom of your heart, and put that prayer rut behind you once and for all.

MOM TO MASTER

Lord, thank You for all of the blessings in my life, but most of all, thank You for just being You. Amen.

Am I Forgotten?

*Then Jesus told his disciples a parable to show them
that they should always pray and not give up.*

LUKE 18:1

Are you waiting for God to answer a very important prayer request? Are you getting weary in praying about this matter? Do you ever feel like God has forgotten you and your request? Well, He hasn't. And He won't. He tells us in Luke 18 that we should always pray and not give up. So, keep praying! Don't give up! Your answer, your ultimate victory, may be right around the corner.

I once interviewed a woman who had always longed to meet her birth father. He left when she was just an infant, and she'd never been able to track him down. She had cried out to God many times to help her in her search. Then, finally, after more than forty years, everything fell into place, and she was reunited with her father. It was a glorious reunion. Immediately, they established the relationship that had been lost due to unfortunate circumstances. God brought them back together, and they are definitely making up for lost time.

This woman shared with me that she never gave up. Every year, she'd say, "This will be the year I'll find Daddy." What if she had quit believing that after only thirty-nine years? So, don't give up. Don't quit. Keep praying because God is still listening and working on your behalf.

MOM TO MASTER
Lord, help me to never give up. Amen.

HEARING THE HEART

If we don't know how or what to pray, it doesn't matter.
He does our praying in and for us, making prayer
out of our wordless sighs, our aching groans.

ROMANS 8:26 MSG

I once read this beautiful statement: "God hears more than words. He listens to the heart," and I've always remembered it. I love that thought. That means even if I can't communicate with words, God knows my heart. He hears my heart cries.

When my best friend had a stillborn baby a few years back, I couldn't get to her that night. I felt a million miles from her, and I wanted to be with her. I cried out to God, but I couldn't figure out what to pray. I was so heartbroken for her and her family. I couldn't believe that the baby we had been preparing for all of those months had already gone to heaven. I couldn't find the words, but the Holy Spirit prayed through me. After a few minutes

of praying, I felt a sort of release. The heaviness
left me, and I knew my friend was going to be
okay. I knew her baby was sitting on the Father's
lap and that someday we'd be able to hold that
precious baby. If you're hurting today and having
trouble knowing what to pray, just cry out to God.
He understands.

MOM TO MASTER
Thank You, Lord, for hearing my heart. Amen.

BRING IT ON!

"That's why I urge you to pray for absolutely everything,
ranging from small to large.
Include everything as you embrace this God-life,
and you'll get God's everything."

MARK 11:24 MSG

Do you pray specifically or do you pray big, broad, general prayers? If you're praying general prayers, you're missing out. God wants us to pray specifically about small and large matters.

He wants us to bring everything to Him, but not all at once. Think of it this way. It'd be like going into a department store and saying to your husband, "Buy me something pretty." You may be longing for a pretty ring, but he buys you a pretty scarf. You didn't get what you wanted because you didn't ask specifically for a pretty ring. It's the same way with God.

Instead of just praying for world peace, why not pray for peace in your home? Instead of only praying for the economy to turn around, why not pray for your family to become debt-free? Instead of praying for your children to be happy, why not pray for your children to walk in the plans that God has for them?

You have to give God something to work with. Be specific. Find Scriptures to stand on. Confess those daily. Praise God for the expected answers to your prayers and get ready for your miracles!

Mom to Master

Thank You, Lord, for being concerned about the big and small things in my life. Amen.

RETREAT AND REPLENISH

*But Jesus Himself would often slip away
to the wilderness and pray.*

LUKE 5:16 NASB

"Retreat and replenish." Remember that phrase? It's helped me a lot over the past few years. Every time I feel I have nothing left to give, Jesus reminds me that it's time to retreat and replenish. By spending time on my knees and in His Word, I am refilled with God's love, power, strength, joy, and energy. I give God all of my worries, sickness, concerns, tiredness, and grouchiness, and He gives me all the good stuff. What a deal, eh? Even Jesus recognized the need to retreat and replenish. After He had healed many people and driven out demons, He needed to retreat and replenish, too.

If you're feeling worn out today, turn to God. Let Him reenergize you. Let Him refuel you with His love so that you'll have love to give your children. As moms, we have to refuel so that we are ready to minister to our families.

As moms, we set the tone for the home. If we're stressed out and drained, our homes will be full of stress and confusion. So, do yourself and your family a favor and retreat and replenish. God is ready to fill you up!

MOM TO MASTER

Lord, fill me up with Your love and strength and joy. I love You. Amen.

In God We Trust

Those who know your name
will trust in you,
for you, LORD, have never forsaken
those who seek you.

PSALM 9:10

Do you trust God? Do you really trust Him? As Christians, we're supposed to trust God. It even says "In God We Trust" on our money. Maybe you trust God in some areas of your life, but you have trouble trusting Him in other areas. That's where I am. I struggle a little bit when it comes to trusting Him with my children. I have to daily declare, "Lord, I trust You with my kids, and I thank You for taking such good care of them today."

It's not that I think I can do a better job than He can. That would be downright ridiculous. I just have trouble giving up control. You see, trusting means giving God your kids. It means giving God all of your worries and fears concerning your kids.

And, it means giving God all of the dreams that you have for your children.

If you're having trouble trusting God with your children, get back in His Word. Read over all of the promises. Hold on to those promises. You can trust Him with everything—even your children.

MOM TO MASTER
Lord, I give my kids to You. I give You all of my worries concerning my kids, and I give You all of the dreams I have for my children. Amen.

GIVING YOUR BEST

"For God so loved the world that
he gave his one and only Son,
that whoever believes in him shall not perish
but have eternal life."

JOHN 3:16

Do you give God your best? Do you give Him your best praise? Do you give Him your best attention? Do you give Him your best effort? Do you give Him your best love?

If you don't, you're not alone. We all fail to give God the very best of ourselves. Instead of giving Him the best that we've got, we offer Him our leftovers.

Especially at this time of year, when giving is such an important part of the holiday season, we need to make sure we're giving God our best. We need for our children to see us giving God our best. Let them see you getting up thirty minutes early in the morning to spend time with God. Let them see you dropping more money into the offering plate. Let them see you praising the Lord at every given opportunity. Let them see you being kind to strangers. If they see you serving God wholeheartedly, they will want to do the same.

Give God your best today. After all, He gave us His very best when He sent Jesus more than two thousand years ago. He certainly deserves our best.

MOM TO MASTER

Heavenly Father, help me to always give You the best of me. Help me to put You first in every situation. I love You. Amen.

WE'RE ONLY HUMAN

"As for God, his way is perfect;
the word of the LORD is flawless.
He is a shield for all who take refuge in him."

2 SAMUEL 22:31

We do the best we can do as Christian moms. Like the Bible says, we train up our children in the ways of the Lord, and we pray for them on a regular basis. We take them to church. We offer words of wisdom whenever the opportunity arises. We try to set a good example for them. But in all of that doing, guess what? Our children will still make mistakes. They will still disappoint us. Why? Because they are only human. And though we like to think our little bundles of joy are perfect, they are far from it. They are no more perfect than we are. That's a scary thought, eh? There's only One who is perfect, and as long as we point our children toward Him, we've done the very best that we can do.

And just as the Master forgives us when we stray, we need to do the same for our kids. We need to be merciful and loving like our heavenly Father. In fact, we need to emulate Jesus so that our kids will want to serve the Lord. So, do your best and let God do the rest!

Mom to Master

Lord, help me to always point my children toward You and Your Word. Amen.

CONSISTENCY IS THE KEY

Jesus Christ is the same yesterday, today, and forever.
HEBREWS 13:8 NLT

Consistency. That's why athletes are so strong and perform so well—they train consistently. Unlike me, they don't run two miles one day and then skip four or five days until they can find time to work out again. It's a part of their daily schedule. Being consistent makes the difference between a casual jogger and an avid runner.

It's the same way in our parenting efforts. If we give unconditional love one day and yell and scream the next day, our kids become confused. If we enforce the rules in one situation and bend the rules the next time, we lose our kids' trust and confidence. If we say one thing and do another, we place doubts in our children's minds. We need consistency in every part of our lives.

Hebrews 13:8 tells us that Jesus Christ is the same yesterday, today, and forever, so He is the ultimate when it comes to consistency. Since we are commanded to be like Him, we have a right to ask God to help us in this area of consistency. The Holy Spirit will help you with this aspect of your parenting. It's not easy. It takes effort, but if you'll commit to being consistent in your parenting, your children will become consistently happier kids.

MOM TO MASTER

Lord, please help me to be consistent as I discipline and love my children. Amen.

THE POWER OF PATIENCE

That you do not become sluggish,
but imitate those who through faith
and patience inherit the promises.

HEBREWS 6:12 NKJV

Patience. Ugh! It's so hard to have patience, isn't it? As mothers, we are doers. Our motto is "Just do it!" We don't wait for somebody else to act on our behalf or take care of the situation. We just press forward and accomplish the task. But what happens when the situation is out of our hands? What happens when we can't solve the problem? That's where patience comes in.

Patience is power—did you know that? It gives us the strength to hold strong when our prayers aren't being answered immediately. Patience undergirds our faith until the miracle is manifested. Maybe you've been praying for your children to come back to God. Maybe you're standing in faith for your child's healing. Maybe you've been praying to conceive another child. Whatever it is, hold fast.

If you have been praying for something for quite some time, and the answer hasn't come, have patience. God hasn't forgotten you. He's heard your prayers. Stand your ground in faith, knowing that your answer is on its way in His perfect timing. Don't give up. Don't back down. Press on in patience.

MOM TO MASTER
Lord, help me to stand in patience until the answer comes. I love You and trust You. Amen.

Meditate on the Master

Do not throw away this confident trust in the Lord,
no matter what happens.
Remember the great reward it brings you!
Patient endurance is what you need now,
so you will continue to do God's will.
Then you will receive all that he has promised.

HEBREWS 10:35–36 NLT

Are you problem-centered or solution-centered? When you look at a glass that is half full of milk, do you see it as half empty or half full? In other words, are you a Polly Positive or a Nelly Negative? Well, if you're feeling more like Nelly than Polly today, let me encourage you with a few promises from the Word of God.

"You are strong, and the word of God lives in you, and you have overcome the evil one" (1 John 2:14).

"But thanks be to God! He gives us the victory through our Lord Jesus Christ" (1 Corinthians 15:57).

" 'What is impossible with men is possible with God' " (Luke 18:27).

You see, no matter what you're facing today, God has given you a promise to handle it. Don't dwell on the problem. Meditate on the Master. He has made you more than a conqueror and has already guaranteed your victory. So, don't fret. Rejoice! You have much to celebrate!

MOM TO MASTER

Father God, help me to become a more positive person. Help me, Lord, to be Word-centered, not problem-centered. Amen.

Head for the Light

Because of that, we have even greater confidence
in the message proclaimed by the prophets.
Pay close attention to what they wrote, for their words
are like a light shining in a dark place—
until the day Christ appears and
his brilliant light shines in your hearts.

2 Peter 1:19 NLT

When my girls were little, they would only sleep in their rooms if the nightlights were plugged in and shining brightly. If the lights wouldn't work, or if I forgot to plug them in, the girls were quick to point out the lack of light in their bedrooms. They would not stay in a room that was without light.

We are people of light. We like light. We're sort of like moths—if a light is on, we're drawn to it. That's a good thing. We should want to head for the light. Of course, Jesus is known as the Light of the World. And Psalm 119:130 says that the entrance of God's Word into our hearts brings the insight we need. In other words, the Word sheds light on every situation we could ever have.

If you're struggling with something today, head for the light! God's Word will shed light on your situation and drive out the darkness of confusion. C'mon, step into the light today.

MOM TO MASTER

Heavenly Father, thank You for the light of Your Word. Help me to turn to Your Word in every situation. Amen.

PRAISE GOD

I will be glad and rejoice in you;
I will sing praise to your name, O Most High.
PSALM 9:2

As the year draws to an end, you're probably reflecting on the past twelve months. It's a good time of year for reminiscing and reflecting, as long as those mind activities don't lead you down the paths of regret and guilt. Hey, we've all made mistakes this year. Yes, even Christian moms occasionally do things that displease the Lord. But don't let those mistakes haunt your holidays. If you've repented for those misdeeds, God has already forgiven them and forgotten them. So, you need to do the same. God says in His Word that He has removed your sin as far as the east is from the west—and that's a long way!

Instead of feeling guilty or regretful over past mistakes, take this time to think on the good things that God did through you and in you and for you this year. Think on all of the miracles He performed on behalf of your family.

If you keep a journal, take a few minutes to read through it, and like the song says, "Look what the Lord has done!" Praise God for the victories—both big and small. Let Him know that you appreciate Him today. Give Him praise today! That's the way to close out one year and begin another—praising God!

MOM TO MASTER
Lord, I praise You for all that You've done and all that You're going to do. Amen.

Award-winning writer **Michelle Medlock Adams** has a diverse resumé featuring inspirational books, a children's picture book, and greeting cards. Her insights have appeared in periodicals across America, including *Today's Christian Woman* and *Guideposts for Kids*. She lives in Fort Worth, Texas, with her husband, two daughters, and a "mini petting zoo."